CIGARETTES
AND SADNESS

GRACE HEMPHILL

Grace Hemphill
Artwork Megan Tyler

Printed Worldwide
First Printing 2023
First Edition 2023

10 9 8 7 6 5 4 3 2 1

*I hope this book gives you something to hold onto
in your darkest hours.*

TABLE OF CONTENTS

CHALK & CHEESE

I hate being resentful.

Green with envy.

Jealousy travelling through my veins,

I'm

    drowsy

Exhausted

of being worn out.

Comparisons. Contrasting.

I'm trying not to be spiteful,

But how can I not?

Two people under the same roof.

Grow into different adults.

I LOVE YOU

Shut up

    Shut up

        Shut up you piece of shit.

            I loathe hearing your name.

                I'm sick of your presence.

                I resent you.

                Do you know that?

        I want it to scorch deep.

    Incinerate your soul.

That I hate you.

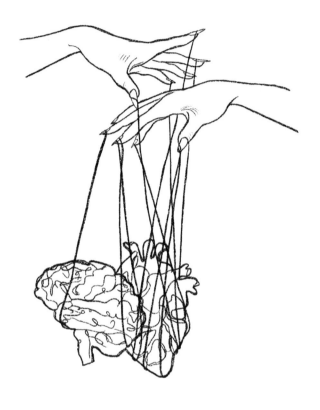

I WANT YOU TO THINK OF ME

I want you to think of me,

Just a blip through your timeline.

When you are getting your morning coffee before work.

Maybe you see someone who looks like me.

And you remember our times.

Think of me when you are in the shower,

At your most vulnerable.

I want you to think of me,

Your curiosity swimming through your blood vessels,

You search the internet,

You want me to be okay,

Even though I shouldn't.

I want you to think of me.

Your sleepless nights,

Your hollow stomach,

Starts to disrupt your existence.

Your fixation grows stronger.

I want you to think of me,

You have turned unstable.

Straitjackets and foam walls are your life.

You are trapped and all you can hear is my name.

I only asked you to think of me.

I only wanted you.

To think of.

Me.

Who knew doing nothing could take up so much time and energy

A Different Fairy Tale

I am only sensational,
Because of my trauma.
Because of my story.
Because I have something to share.

Once it is distributed
I am a shell of a human
A meaningless encounter

I am only attractive,
Because of my miscalculations.

My agony

My terror

I'm who I am because of the summer months,
When I was sixteen,
And I thought,
I was in love.

MOTHER

I cannot wait to cradle you.

But the thought of you.

Puts panic into my heart.

Will I be able to love you?

The way you need to be loved?

Will I be able to make you

Mine?

The thought of you,

Makes me icy with sadness.

I don't want you to drown,

In my misery.

TIRED

I am

Consumed.

Physically drained,

Of all my resources.

My eyelids

Heavy.

With each

Blink.

Shivering.

Quivering.

Coldness overwhelms me.

Let me sleep.

Let

Me

Go.

I talk to the moon and he tells me stories about the sun

THIS ISN'T A LOVE POEM

Love poems
don't have
to be about
people.
They can be about
that first
sip
of your coffee in
the morning.
It can be about
that skirt,
that gives you an
increase in
self-confidence.
You can
talk about the book,
that made
you cry happy tears.
You can
write about the day
you accepted yourself.
For who
you were
And
nothing
less.

READ BETWEEN MY LINES

I don't want to be loved unconditionally.

I want to be shown when I am treating you less than you deserve.

I want you to leave,

If I even start.

Making you promises I do not

Commit to.

Love me for my flaws but don't let them hurt you.

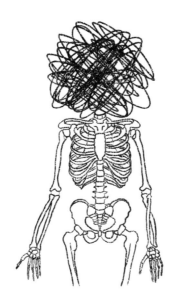

Pretty face with pretty bad dreams

EVIDENCE

Maybe if you left me,

Bruised and bleeding.

I would have been able to ask for help.

But you only wounded me enough to feel.

It on the inside.

You selfish bastard

My words against yours,

Your hands against me,

Your shouts and my cries.

Your insecurities against my naivety.

My innocence.

DREAMS

I dreamt of you last night.

I was running,

        Running.

              Running.

                    Away.

Yet I always managed to run into

You.

Excitement and fear fuelled me.

I wanted to stay there,

But daylight took me home.

STONE COLD

It has been six years.

And I still remember every word.

You said to me.

Every time you touched me.

Every place you made me feel cold.

I still remember your hazel eyes.

Staring back at me.

Emptiness.

No lights on inside your eyes.

Yet I'm the mad one.

Don't try to put me on a pedestal

I'm afraid of heights

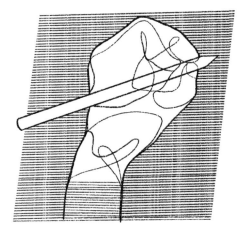

WRITER'S BLOCK

I want to write.

But the words won't come to my fingertips.

I'm
trying to find
the colours.

But everything is grey.

I was a painting but you were.

Colour-blind.

HEARTLESS

Take my heart,

I don't think I need it,

And I trust you enough to look after it.

As serious as a heart attack

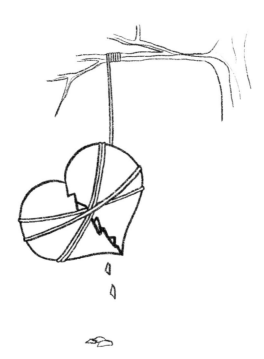

My Muse

I hate the power you have over me.

You are in my dreams.

Disrupting my sleep.

Certain TV shows make me think of.

you.

I can no longer enjoy life.

The way I am meant to

I am sick of writing metaphors about you

90s Mixtape

All the songs,

We used to listen to.

I wanted you to listen,

To the lyrics.

I was dyslexically in love with you.

All the feelings, none of the words.

Those meant the world to me.

And you were deaf.

Drink the poison lightly.

IMMATURE

I wanted to have your baby,

All whilst you wanted to have my innocence.

Put it in a jar on the shelf with the rest.

Something you can gratify yourself to.

You didn't love me.

You loved the idea of having me.

Being the first to step on the map.

But you couldn't tame the waves.

CONTROL

I tolerated what you did to me because I thought there was something
better in the future. Fresh green lawn and a white picket fence. I let you
walk over me. I let you belittle me. I didn't even want a green lawn or
picket fence. I became your doormat because I thought you would
one day promote me to the coffee table. I'm only ever useful if I'm on the
floor. Vulnerable. Below you.

SICKNESS

I put hand sanitiser

On my cuts to feel

Something more powerful

Than my own thoughts.

INSANITY

I don't want to hear your voice.

But I want to see your name.

Pop up on my phone.

Love feels like a slap across the face

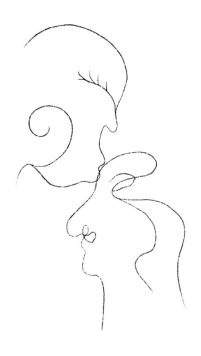

LOCKED DOWN

Baggy clothes,

Mask,

Eyes.

Don't look at my eyes.

Not into my eyes.

I didn't open the door.

So you knocked it down.

I didn't ask for your stare.

I am meant to be invisible.

ELECTRICITY

The static speaks my mind.

The darkness feels safer than outside.

Silence screams I need the TV hiccups.

To soothe me from this place.

Boys are place holders

Girls are forever

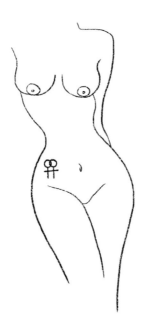

TROPHY WIFE

I spent so long pretending,
To be the girl everyone would want.
Relaxed and predictable,
Definitely not emotional.
Oh please walk all over me.
I won't mind.
Constantly quiet,
But constantly there and reactive.
With the perfect figure,
Minus the imperfect mind.
But because I was what you wanted
And not what you needed.
I was never the one,
You showed off to your parents.
I was the thing,
That made your friends jealous.
I was your legendary status,
I was pleasure walking on a pair of legs,
Play toy.
A TV show you could watch,
When you were tired and brain dead.
I was easy.
To understand.
An open book.
Or so you thought.
Then I got scratched.
So now you need a replacement,

You were not too upset.
Because I was cheap.
I was just relieved to take off my
Mask.
Imagine if it was your sister,
Your daughter,
Your mother,
Your wife.
But it wasn't.
It was me.
Do I not deserve,
Everyone's sympathy?

INNOCENCE

You can't ask for forgiveness.

If you don't choose to accept,

Responsibility for your actions.

You were young,

You didn't know better.

I was also young.

Got it all ripped away from me,

Like a plaster.

All because you didn't understand,

Body language.

I didn't know what had happened,

Until it was too late.

I was too young to know,

The power.

I'm so very tired

And I can't seem to find the monster that is stealing my energy

PROTECT THE LITTLE GIRLS

I'm so terrified of having a little girl,

I would want her to have freedom.

But also protect her.

And to let her know the bad people,

Of the world.

But not to completely scare her.

I would want her to enjoy life,

Without being terrified

Every time she turns a corner.

I want her to stay innocent,

But not to be naïve.

To be open-minded but to,

Know not everyone is worthy,

Of her trust.

SHADES OF BLUE

A little bit of blue

Can be good

A little bit of appreciation

Can go a long way

I appreciate your existence.

Were you beautiful before your cocoon?

CURED OF MY DISEASE

Happy pills,

Doctor's appointments,

Try this,

Drink that,

Like Alice in Wonderland.

Shrink small enough for the door,

Inside your head.

Write your feelings down,

On paper,

And then burn it all,

You are better now.

Get up, get dressed.

You are lazy, not ill.

I can't see it so I can't understand it.

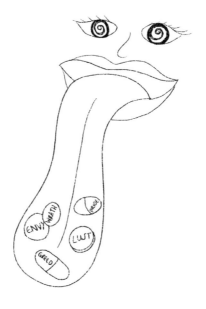

NOISES

Piano chords in my brain.

Keeps me in tune.

Can you hear them too?

Don't let the piano drown you.

Too much noise gives me headaches.

The bridge of my nose.

Tense and painful.

Eyes burning.

Sleep comforts me for now.

But what about the morning?

My writing is drunk.

I hear a noise on my window

And I still go looking for your car outside

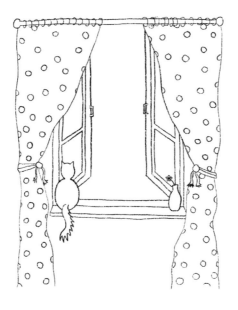

THE TASTE OF TEARS

A wave of sadness washes over me.

I'm drowning.

I can't breathe.

And yet it won't end.

My lungs slowly start to burn,

As they fill with salty water.

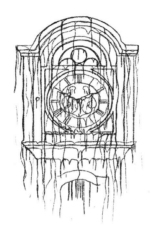

Ticking Time Bomb

Time flies so fast.

I miss out on hours,

Days,

Weeks.

Because I'm scared of getting older.

I'm still a child and I want to scream.

But no one can hear me,

Scream.

Can anyone hear me,

I shout into an empty void.

Was insanity just a matter of dropping the act?

Unexplained Symptoms

I wish you had hurt me,

More.

Maybe I'd have more of,

A story to tell.

More of a reason,

To feel sad.

MIRRORS OF FRAUD

I want to be pretty.

If I can pinch it, it must disappear

I chant in the mirror.

Will you notice me.

If I become small and fragile.

Pathetic and useless.

Quiet and timid.

I may be strong but that doesn't mean,

I don't need your help.

Don't leave me here.

Music helps me find the words I want to say

THERAPY

I hide behind my humour.

Try my best to laugh at a situation,

Otherwise I'll cry.

And if I start,

I won't be able to,

Stop.

Where are the tears stored when they aren't in use?

Or am I out of stock until the,

Foreseeable future.

HIS SCENT

It was my birthday.

The first birthday since we broke

Up.

But we were sat drinking coffee.

And you gave me a hoodie.

And for a brief second I thought it was the past

Again.

The smell of your aftershave,

Drifted through me into my lungs.

I looked you deep in your eyes,

To see if you noticed.

Control.

Was the one thing.

You could use.

At a moment's notice.

Over the course of our love.

You kept little nuggets of information.

To use.

In times.

Of need.

You continued to talk about the others,

Like we had never been intimate.

But I could see through your eyes,

That those girls,

And those nights,

Never gave you happiness.

Like I did.

You purposely made me feel like I was forgotten,

With your words.

But your actions spoke volumes.

Why did you leave your scent?

On a piece of clothing,

I had to take home?

It poisoned my wardrobe.

For months.

And all I could smell was you,

On my jeans.

And in my room.

And I couldn't sleep.

For months,

I was choking on your scent.

As it lived in my room.

No matter how many candles,

I lit up.

It wouldn't leave.

But you are gone from my life.

Now.

And so is that hoodie.

I'm sorry for wasting your time I thought I was fixed

PREMATURE

When I was born I was a month early,

Small and fragile.

Anxious to explore the world.

If I was an animal,

I would have been the runt.

And potentially wouldn't have survived.

I was struggling to breathe.

And I was the wrong weight.

The wrong size.

I was impatient.

And claustrophobic.

I wasn't born the natural way,

I was removed.

Synesthesia

I hear colours,

I see music,

I taste your laughter.

Who was I an hour ago?

Dancing,

Away the night,

Until we see the sunrise,

I can feel all my senses.

I see stars in your eyes

I wish you could see the stars in mine

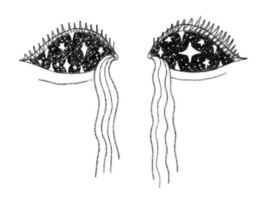

YOU CAN'T CONTROL ME

I wish I had noted down the day,

The time,

The hour.

I stopped listening,

To the voices in my head.

DROWNING

I'm swimming in the ocean,
Of you.
But some days,
I'm fighting against the waves.
Overwhelmingly,
Drowning.
Like there are weights,
Attached to my ankles,
Dragging
me
down.

      My eyes are burning,
         From the chemicals,
            Surrounded by the salty water,
              You can't see my tears,
                It hurts to love you,
                  Like I'm hidden at
            the bottom,
                        Of
                        the
                        ocean

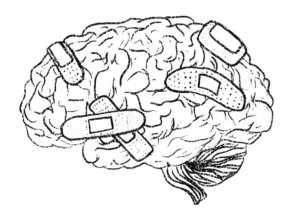

I wish I could put a plaster on my brain to help it heal.

~ 73 ~

Amsterdam

It is like walking on clouds,

And my head feels heavy,

On my shoulders,

But the rest of me is,

W e i g h t l e s s

YOUR SONG

Meeting you was like listening to a song,

> for the first time and
> knowing it would be my
> favourite.

At first, I didn't understand the lyrics.

> But the beat
> intrigued me,

And soon it was the only song I was listening to.

When your past is so present

How can there be a future?

I Want to Talk About Me

When people ask about my story,

I want to get to the stage,

When I don't have to mention your name,

Anymore.

You were never part of me,

Yet I let you define me,

Fuck you for making me,

Feel as if I couldn't be,

Anything more than your shadow.

TOMORROW

It is hard to explain that you don't want to live to the person who
gave me the ability to exist. You have heard of the metaphors. The
dark cloud. The grey dog. But it is more than that. It doesn't just
follow me. It is inside of me. It is like being possessed by a demon.
Don't be scared. I'm harmless. I don't want to die. But I don't want
to live. Let me sleep a little longer. It is hard to explain. What is
going on inside my head. When I barely know myself. I'm
frightened to wake up. What version of me will I see in the mirror?
Will I sleep. Will I cry. Will I feel the urge to hurt myself. Just
because he used to. You want me to meditate? I laugh. The voices in
my head won't shut up. Make me a cup of tea. I'll try again
tomorrow.

I left the house today and it wasn't with you

WHAT IS LOVE?

You have the ability to absolutely destroy me,

And I'm trusting you not to.

Isn't that all love is?

Love is the butterflies I feel,

When I see your green eyes.

I hope our children get your eyes,

Mysterious like the sea.

What are you hiding?

FLYING TO NEVERLAND

As a young girl,

I used to dream,

About flying,

About having a house,

Made of clouds,

White, soft, bouncy,

I felt safe up there,

When life got scary,

I would fly up there,

It makes me wonder,

If in a previous life,

I was a bird; a crow,

I always did feel myself,

With my black hair,

A black, beautiful crow,

Maybe there is a timeline,

Out there,

Where I can fly.

I'm in love with cities I've never been to and people never met

Boomerang

One minute it was bliss.
I felt loved and appreciated.
The next moment, I was the prize.
The pretty girl on your arm.
You got angry at me,
For being imperfect,
Because I had a beautiful face,
But not a beautiful mind.

That confused you.

You tried to fix me,
But I didn't want to be fixed.

I screamed at you.
Until I was blue in the face.

And months later you are chasing me again.
Like you have forgotten the definition of,
Insanity.

INTOXICATED

Drunk consciousness.

Friends.

More.

Voices in my head.

Take me to bed.

Surface level me.

And not underneath the sea.

Iceberg.

Use my generosity as flirting.

I don't like the colour green.

But I fell in love with your eyes.

She got the good side of you

Bubble Bath

W a v e s upon waves,

Of e c s t a s y.

D a n c i n g on the ceiling,

Moving with the r h y t h m.

Of the water,

S e n s u a l awakening.

Relaxation,

Tension l e t g o.

Floating,

Feeling weightless on the w a t e r .

PAIN & PLEASURE

Tell me that you love me.

                With your hand around my neck.

Look deep into my eyes.

I want to see your pupils.

Dilate.

                With the thought of me.

                    Connected.

         As one.

I'm a girl standing in a tornado

Pretending like it isn't even windy

Maneater

Curves,
Of seduction.

Intimidation.

Promiscuity.

She is dangerous.

Mysterious,
Like the night.

She is quiet,
But loud when she wants to be.

Don't catch her staring at you.

She will kill you with just,
Her eyes.

FEMININITY

Love me.

Hate me.

I will still undress you,

With my eyes.

Hate that you love me.

Love that you hate me.

I'm in charge,

Powerful.

Controlling.

I'm the chaos you couldn't control

First Date

You want to get to know me.
Don't ask me about my star sign.
Ask me about the first time I fell in love.
Ask me why I'm always tired.
Ask me what I dream about.
Ask me why I pick the skin from my lips,
Even when I start to bleed.
Ask me about my scars.
Ask me how many pills I have to take,
Just to feel an ounce of normality.
Ask me why I drink coffee.
Ask me why I drink wine.
Ask me when I knew I loved women,
And how much that scared me.
Ask me why I like the idea of being sectioned.
Ask me about what makes me cry.
Ask me about what makes me laugh.
Don't ask me about my favourite colour,
When I see the world in black and white.
Ask me what makes me angry.
Ask me why I always feel lonely,
In a room full of people.
Ask me why I wrote this poem.

Cup of Coffee

I'm not everyone's cup of tea,
Which is fine,
Because I don't even like tea,
Maybe I can be your cup of coffee?
Bitter,
And dark,
I keep you up at night,
But you need me to survive the day,
You are addicted to me,
How many cups will you have today?
I make you think,
I can be whatever version you want me to be,
You crave different things on different days,
Even though you'll always have a favourite side of me,
I cause you to shake if you have too much of me,
But I cause headaches if I'm not there enough.
I'm the first thought you have,
As soon as you wake up.
You won't admit that you're addicted,
To me.

I wanna look at you and feel at home

Welcome to my brain, Welcome to my home.

I'm sorry I didn't tidy up.

I didn't expect anyone to come.

There is a book shelf over there,

Full of all the fictional worlds and characters,

I would rather be living in.

And there are drawers full of ideas,

For stories and books,

That I have never finished,

Or never even started.

And there is my record player,

With music ready for any mood.

And there are bean bags.

And coffee.

And pretty LED lights that change colour.

Everything works in its own section when I'm in a good mood.

But when I'm not,

Rain   pours   through   the

ceiling.

Causing   the   lights   to   turn   off.

The   records   all have   scratches   on them,

And   all   I   hear   is

noise.

All the   stories get   mixed   up

and   none   of   them   have   happy   endings.

And   everything   is   flooded,

And   I   feel   like   I'm

drowning.

Teenage Dream

Remember when you were 15 and you thought you wanted a bad boy.

And then you managed to get yourself one.

And he left you there crying in the woods.

Because you wouldn't pull your trousers down.

He told you he loved you.

And guilted you into loving him with your body.

He loved you in the dark.

Behind closed doors.

I spent so long.

Losing myself.

Thinking it would help you stay.

You emptied my bottle.

And then runaway.

Onto your next adventure.

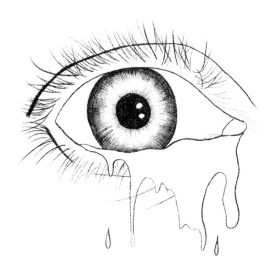

Sometimes I hate everyone but you

And other times you are the only human being I despise with such fire red passion

Driving Anxiety

I'm scared to learn to   drive.

To be in   control of an   unpredictable,

Vehicle.

Nervous of

r o u n d a b o u t s.

Of tight country roads.

I prefer trains.

Where I can write.

      Read.

      Think.

      Feel.

TEARS OF GROWTH

I have been abused.

And been the abuser.

I have been used.

And the user.

I have been betrayed.

And betrayed someone else.

I have been lied to.

And also been a liar.

With everything I knew,

And experienced.

Why did I still enjoy myself?

We will meet again beyond the indecision

Wrong Timing

Maybe in an alternate universe.

We are together,

Where our personalities don't clash.

Where I treat you better.

If I knew what was wrong,

With me.

I could teach you how I work.

But I don't know that either.

OUT OF STORIES

Blank page

Twitching fingers

Aching hands

Have I finished writing my story about you?
If I no longer think of you.
Who fills my mind?
I've been dried up

Of all my creativity.
The light has stopped working in my head.
It is empty,
And cold.

What do I focus on now?
What is my purpose

Without the trauma?

If loving you means anything than doing it fully then count me out

CHEMICAL IMBALANCE

Drugs, drugs, drugs
Not the fun kind.

You take at a party,
To release your anxiety.

The kind that blocks your brain.
From all it can feel.

Everything is black and white

Do I remember what your green eyes look like?

I miss being creative

I didn't want to feel,
But now nothing enters my brain.
What even is an original idea?
I want to be able to just write away the day,
But I'm numb to creativity.

Cognitive Behaviour

20 years of tragic mistakes

Unlearnt behaviours

A broken system

Like I'm stuck

Saving documents

On a floppy disk

I will forever remain obsessed and addicted to you

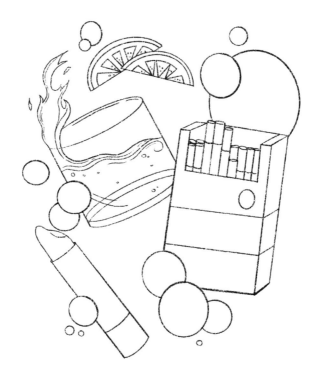

BAG OF BONES

I'm tired of hurting.

Of waking every day.

Still in pain.

Life is too short.

But my brain won't.

Kick you out.

PLOT TWIST

I asked the universe for a heartbreak.

I just didn't expect you to be the one to make me heartbroken.

You can now be included in my book of hurt.

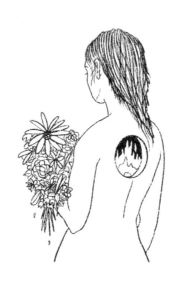

I know I love you

but I don't recognise you.

I MISS HER

Quiet girl with the sad eyes,

Tears engraved on her face.

Because she has run out of tissues,

Of words to say to make her easier to understand.

Other writers have managed to capture

All her thoughts in words that she didn't know

Existed.

Lyrics form her story

Her body may be here

But her mind is miles away

Bring her back home to me,

I miss her.

Sand Between my Fingers

I had a dream where,

      I was listening to music I'd never

            Heard before.

        I can't remember

What your face looks like

      How much time has

          Passed?

          How many

hourglasses

      Have been turned?

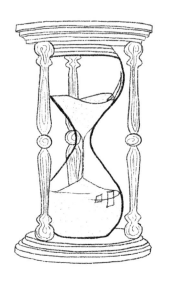

The old man who smells of cigarettes and sadness

PHOTOGRAPHIC

The camera can't quite,

Capture how beautiful,

Your eyes are.

The way they shine among,

The darkness.

Lighting up the winter,

Morning sky.

Not sure what colour,

They want to be.

Are they swimming with the ocean?

Or swaying with the trees?

And even when there is a stormy cloud,

Over your head your eyes shine,

Through.

You don't want to love me You want to have power over me I will no longer allow you to make me feel small

STRANGER IN THE SHADOWS

I know when I'm getting bad again

You start to show up in places

You would never be

I'm hoping you wouldn't recognise me

I've changed enough to no longer be

Something you're interested in

PEOPLE PLEASER

Don't fix yourself, until you're perfect.

For perfect doesn't exist.

And your loved ones would have to,

Adjust to the new you.

When they are happy,

With you.

Now.

Even if you're not.

Alphabetical Madness

There are 26 letters

I am allowed

To combine

To describe

How you

Make me

Feel

Red Wine

The first time I had red wine.

I was sat across the table.

From you.

We spent the evening.

Pretending to be grown ups.

Talking and laughing the evening away.

like we had the future planned together.

We went our separate ways and.

Now I drink.
Red wine alone.
Laughing with the shadows in my.
Room.

I wish for future female generations to be able to walk through the darkness without fear overtaking them

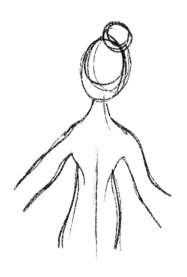

RED MEANS SCARY

Daisies don't compare to a rose.

All flowers are beautiful in their own way.

And maybe daisies make you smile.

Whereas a rose makes you commit.

Red with passion and love.

White and yellow with childish intentions.

Around the wrist of a little girl.

I FIND COMFORT IN DEATH

I want to be

so close to

death I want to

feel death but

not experience it

I want to be friends

with death let him

hold my hands

talk to him

death with benefits

Blood Loss

If it was only a

Paper cut.

Maybe I wouldn't,

Have minded.

A paper cut on my heart.

A little bit of fear is okay

But a lot can be debilitating

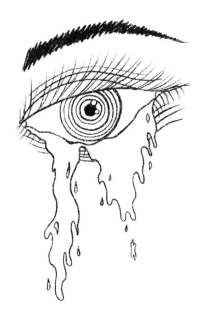

AFRAID

I like to think I'm a wolf.

Covered in scars.

But ready to conquer the world.

Day after day.

But I'm more like a deer.

Constantly

running

Constantly

on

edge

Afraid

of

staying

still

For

Too

Long

Mansion Hoarder

Ah to be rich and lonely.

to not think you need.

anyone.

in your empty house.

the empty space in your body.

where your heart used to be.

Growing pains

I need you to tell me things

I already know

Otherwise I

can't help you.

ABOUT THE AUTHOR

Grace Hemphill is an introspective poet whose heartfelt verses delve into the depths of mental illness, with a focus on themes of depression and anxiety. She has passionately been writing poetry since the age of 16, using her words to explore the complexities of the human mind and emotions.

Her poetry captures the raw essence of her personal experiences and resonates with readers who have faced similar struggles. Each poem sheds light on her own inner battles and the moments she has struggled through, while also revealing a glimmer of hope amidst the darkness.

With her book, Grace aims to offer empathy and understanding to anyone else who grapples with mental illness. This collection of poetry marks her third publication, following the release of "Letters to my Past" in 2017 and "Thoughts of a Depressed Human" in 2020.

Printed in Great Britain
by Amazon